HELENA —
Happy to sharing
Poetry at
the manor

Marty Gervais

Meeting Thoreau at the Gas Station Diner

by Marty Gervais

Crossroads Poetry Series
Three Fires Confederacy
Waawiiyaatanong ✦ Windsor, ON

First Edition. April 2022

Library and Archives Canada Cataloguing in Publication

Title: Meeting Thoreau at the gas station diner / by Marty Gervais.
Names: Gervais, C. H. (Charles Henry), 1946- author.
Series: Crossroads poetry series.
Description: Series statement: Crossroads poetry series | Poems.
Identifiers: Canadiana 20220196222 | ISBN 9781988214481 (softcover)
Classification: LCC PS8563.E7 M44 2022 | DDC C811/.54—dc23

Book cover design: D.A. Lockhart
Cover Image: Steve Shook "Marnye's Standard Service, 1950 - Hammond, Indiana"
Author Photo: Ted Gervais
Book layout: D.A. Lockhart

Published in the United States of America and Canada by

 Urban Farmhouse Press
www.urbanfarmhousepress.ca

The Crossroads Poetry Series is a line of books that showcases established and emerging poetic voices from across North America. The books in this series represent what the editors at UFP believe to be some of the strongest voices in both American and Canadian poetics.

Printed in Adobe Garamond Pro

The world is but a canvas to our imagination.
Henry David Thoreau

Contents

Introduction: From Sea to Sea: Marty Gervais' Journey

A year had passed since the summer of love. 1968, the summer of heartbreaks and assassinations, a time of new experiences, the end of innocence, and the beginning of a new journey. The summer of love saw the assassinations of Martin Luther King Jr., Robert F. Kennedy, and the passing of two famous travelers, Neal Cassady of *On the Road* fame and the novelist John Steinbeck. It was a time of disillusionment and a time of discovery. For some, it was the psychedelic summer, while for others such as Marty Gervais it was the summer when poetry became a way of finding what had been lost.

In 1968, Marty Gervais set off in search of the country of his birth. His journey took him from sea to sea as he lived the Canadian motto, ad mare usque ad mare. What he found between the oceans was not merely geography but the people who inhabited that space, the human spirit that did not, in the words of Northrop Frye ask the question "Where is here?" but wondered "Who is here and why?"

On his journey from coast to coast, Gervais was guided by his spiritual mentors, though in spirit only, the poet Thomas Merton and the ghost of another American writer, Henry David Thoreau who found himself in the silences and stillness of a Concord, Massachusetts pond. They both shared one overwhelming curiosity that became the hallmark of Gervais' work as a journalist and as a poet and writer. That curiosity found its *metier* in his natural inclination to discover not just the people but the stories they lived.

Unlike Thoreau and Merton, Gervais has never shied away from the world. He is engaged by it. His chief desire is to know people, not just places, the experience those who live their own stories and search for their own explanations for the absurdity and complexity of the world by striking out in the world – more Franciscan than Benedictine in its pursuit. The world, as Gervais learned in the summer after the summer of love, remained a puzzling and intriguing place where love and pity, joy and curiosity, are still the operative principles others live by. He could no more leave the world behind for the cloister or the woodland pond than he could cease his need to explore.

The poems in this volume are more than chronicles. They reveal the story of a young man who wanted to move through society to understand what makes the society of a country live and breathe. In many ways, the summer of 1968 shaped the poet Marty Gervais would become in the ensuing decades – the poet driven by a profound curiosity in people. And perhaps that is what still unites this country, despite its layers of brutality and silence that have only recently come to light. People, Gervais concludes, are still relatively good even when they are not aware of the history they are living.

From one coast to the other, and back to the City of Windsor where he had been born but had not lived until his journey in 1968 brought him full-circle, people are fascinating. They learn, they work, and they love, and each in their own way is unique. And when the journey was done and new horizons appeared for both his travels and his personal life, he found himself where he began in a way that is reminiscent of Dorothy's famous lines from the conclusion of *The Wizard of Oz*: that if I ever go looking for my heart's desire I will never look farther than my own backyard.

In this respect, *Meeting Thoreau at the Gas Station Diner* is a kind of *Odyssey* where the protagonist travels not merely to learn about others and where they live but, as Freud said, to pass from unconsciousness into a state of waking. These poems are about a young traveler who wakes from his past only to discover that his journey has brought him home.

Bruce Meyer, December 2021
Barrie, Ontario, Canada

PROLOGUE

That Summer on the Road

I found out about Martin Luther King
being shot that day when I set out
to hitch a ride home to Muskoka
I hadn't been standing any more than
a few minutes along the highway when
a raven-black Thunderbird with its gaping
grille mouth and hideway headlamps
pulled up and I raced to catch up and
open the side door and hop in, settling down
in the back and noticed the driver's mug
in the side view mirror as he peered through the window
before swerving back onto the highway
the whole time firing a volley of questions
wondering where I was headed,
where I was coming from, and before I could
say anything he was talking a mile-a-minute
to the woman beside him in the front
a passenger who had kicked off her shoes
and there in the back next to me but hugging
the window was another woman
wearing a tie-dye headband
and still, I hadn't said a word but now
we were on our way —the start of a journey
I was only beginning to imagine, and soon
the driver was asking me again where I was going
and again before I could tell him
I was headed to Bracebridge he announced
they were driving to Regina.
I had 65 cents in my pocket but right
there and then I said, "Oh, yeah, that's
where I'm headed…" And so, it began
this ride across the country
All I had with me was a knapsack
with a notebook, a paperback
of Gary Snyder's Back Country,
Thoreau's Walden,
a toothbrush and wool-knit sweater

I was 21 bound for my parent's home
to pull my life back together after a breakup
with a woman I'd been living with
and a job at the Globe & Mail
It wasn't until we were passing
through Thunder Bay, already dark
as we slipped by sleepy neighbourhood porches
and flickering lights of night time diners
and that's when I heard the news on the car radio
about Martin Luther King being shot dead
on a balcony outside his second-floor room
at the Lorraine Motel in Memphis
and the four of us fell silent in the car
listening to the news, and the blunt
and endless refrain of the wipers
on the rainy windshield.

"We do not take a trip; a trip takes us..." —John Steinbeck

Goodbye Hello

I opened my eyes on a couch in Regina —
being shaken awake by the boyfriend
of the woman from the back seat of the car
that took me west

It annoyed his family that I'd tagged
along with the bride their son was about to marry
I was told to collect my things
I'd be driven to the highway

He wanted to drive me as far away as possible

I climbed into the backseat of the father's car
and we were just pulling away when the girlfriend
raced from the steps of the house demanding
to know what was going on — and swung open
the passenger door, and hopped in
right beside me

I saw the look on her boyfriend's face
—now here I was riding in the backseat
along with his girlfriend as I had
for 1,600 miles from Toronto
not to say anything of nights in hotels

and we rode in silence seven or eight miles
out of Regina—sweep of the flat open highway
and the sun edging awake in a haze, and now
alone, poised on the highway
shivering in the cold, and not a car in sight
except theirs on his broad, flat treeless plain
and I watched it do a U-ie, and start back
to the city when abruptly it braked in the middle
of the road, and sat there for an eternity
the faint exhaust pipe rattle in the crisp prairie air
and a door popped opened
and the girlfriend raced back to throw her arms

around me, nearly knocking me over
and planted a hard kiss on my cheek then
straightened up, composed herself, promptly
handed me at $20 bill like she owed it to me
and whispered *I hope you make it!*

PS: She sent me a picture of her wedding two months later

Full Moon on a Sunday

I got as far as Moose Jaw but hitched
a ride to the outskirts and it was getting
dark, and I eyed a young boy
with his father whose truck was parked
in a nearby field just off the road
— the kid was setting up
and fiddling with a sleek telescope on a stand
working the eyepiece to fix the focus
of the full moon, and the chances
of getting a ride now were pretty slim
I sauntered over crossing the tall grass
to strike up a conversation with the two
 – and in a few minutes it was my eyes now
studying the April moon
so high in the cold prairie sky
I didn't know what to say
when the boy rattled on about dead
volcanoes, impact craters, lava flows
and the dark surface stretches being oceans
and I knew none of this really
though I remembered my brother
building a telescope, spending an entire summer
during the 1950s, grinding and polishing
the glass, assembling it into a long tube
then slapping together a clapboard observatory
from discarded crates in the side lot
of our house in Windsor
I told the boy this, and here we were
48 miles west of Regina
lounging in a plain jane pasture
under a cloudless sky, our sights
on a moon that lit up this empty field
and the not-so-far distant town
and after a while, the father advised his son
to pack up, that they were heading home
but before he slipped into his truck
to depart, he paused and returned
to warn me to stay awake — he knew

it was unlucky to sleep in the moonlight
but especially with a full moon
on a Sunday, and though I scoffed
at such silly superstitions, I still paced
a short stretch of that highway
for hours till a short-order cook
on his way to work picked me up
and I spent the rest of the night
slumped in a booth of his all-night diner
thankful for him whipping up a plate
of ham and eggs and letting me sit
and read the morning paper and silently
pray for the first rays of daylight

First Hearing Gordon Lightfoot

That early spring of 1968
on a cool Saskatchewan night
I paced the edge of the highway
daydreaming the sweep of open fields

certainly praying under an ink-black sky
that rested solitary and present over me
like the palm of a hand

when a preacher swerved
to the side of the road
in a dusty green Plymouth Belvedere

I spotted the flashing red ribbon taillights
that wrapped around the knife-edge crease
running down to the bumper
and heard the man shout if I needed a ride

I hopped in, eager to be on my way
and talk soon turned to Jesus
and forgiveness and morality
and the Psalms
and I asked if he could turn on the radio

That's when I first heard that voice
sailing up and out this preacher's car —
a voice that spun in the still prairie air
the blur of notes like the landscape
whistling by

and I told him to turn up the radio
and that he'd have to stop talking and listen
and said if the apostles had this man's voice
there'd be real hope to cling to

and we wound the windows shut
and grew silent in that precipitous moment
feeling the highway stretch clean and straight
beneath us murmuring as endless prayer

An Alphabet of Love

I heard it first — that indistinct faraway
muffle and sputter of an old plane, and I turned
sharply around from where I was standing on the highway
to spot this old WWII Spitfire dip down
over the nearby village — its high-pitch roar
once described as a symphony of 12 cylinders
waking up afternoon shopkeepers and businessmen
and as the plane steadied and slowed over the main drag
that day, you could easily gaze up and make out
the lengthy train of letters it dragged behind
— its words clearly declaring
Billie, I love you more than my mother!
I didn't know Billie, didn't know if this was a man
or a woman, a suitor, a brother or friend
if this was a plea, an argument looking
for a satisfying finish, but there I was reading
the banner with its seven-foot letters as it wove
in and out of the blue sky, and I half-felt
I'd like to lift up and take hold and ride that sentiment
— we all want to be loved

Boxcars in Swift Current

I scrambled up on a scrappy red
20-ton CN boxcar, its tall doors open
and sat down on its wide flat wooden floor
just about the time the sun was going down
then felt the whole line of cars shift
and move and figured I was on my way
but in a matter of moments
was sliding off to a siding to sit and watch
the darkness collect, and a yardman walked past
and smiled but didn't say anything
and so all this romance of riding boxcars
across the prairie grassland
evaporated and I waited till the cars
finally stopped, and jumped down
and made my way back to the yard
and spotted the switchman making his way
toward me, smiling again, and now
shaking his head, and hearing his words
Where are you going? And I said I'd hoped
to make it to the coast, and he turned away
and with a wave of his left arm to follow him
I watched and trailed after him to a pickup—
in one gloved hand, he held a tin lunch pail
and he turned again to face me
as he opened the door and said for me
to jump in, and he'd take me back
to the highway, and there was nothing
no other choice — I'd have a better
chance hitching a ride there
and when he pulled over
to the shoulder of the Trans-Canada
he reached over and unlatched the lunch box
and pulled out a mickey, and offered it
and it burned all the way down
in my chest like the sun

The Chevy Bel Air in Medicine Hat

The best ride ever —somehow I hoped
it would be when I saw this dreamy Chevy Bel Air
slow down and cruise toward me
in the early morning sunlight
and I caught the driver in a stiff straw hat
nod for me to hop in, and I dropped
into the soft leather seats, turquoise, and white
like the dashboard, and he could tell
I was impressed, but the man never
took his eyes off the road as he told me
this was a 1954 two-door coupe
and *didn't I like it* ….but I wasn't
really listening — I could barely hear
the car hum, nearly silent, as we made
our way west to Maple Creek
and the man went on endlessly
about how he had bought it brand new
with money saved by moving in
and taking care of his aging mother
and now that she had passed he hoped
to marry the woman he was about
to meet up with, someone he'd known
for more than a year, and how
she reminded him of his mother
maybe the way she listened, or the way
she sat attentive with hands cupped on her lap
and his plan was to take his sweetheart
for a ride in the Bel Air, down to the river
and park under the Dogwoods and propose
to her, and *what did I think of that* and so
I wished him all the luck in the world
and when we drove into Maple Creek
past the tall straight storefronts
I thought he was going to drop me off
but first, he wanted to show me where
he was going to take his bride, then guided
the big car down to the river and we sat
under the dogwoods, and he reached
into the back for a bouquet of flowers

and said *What do you think? Is this a good idea?*
And what could I say?
He had driven me 132 miles

Backpack

I never much liked carrying anything
except this tidy backpack with two books
and later a toothbrush
an extra sweater
a lined notebook
anything else

stuffed into the canvas bag
like a few extra rolls of toilet paper
from a gas station

I could've used a sleeping bag
a warmer jacket
a decent pair of shoes
just about anything

but it was all fine —
how much more content could I be
than to scramble up
the morning highway after a night
of bedding down under a blinking Milky Way
25,000 light-years away?

Midnight in Banff

I had all the luck in the world
especially catching a ride just outside Calgary
 — nightfall, and a lawyer heading home to Banff
swerved over in his sea-green Mercedes

I had been at this all day and as I sank
into the plush leather seat, I promptly
fell asleep, dreaming I was still
on the road under a hot prairie sun

and when I woke, we were cruising
along Banff Avenue, the main drag
and the man smiled just as I opened my eyes
and I apologized for not staying awake

All fine, he said —we were there
and the man braked in front of a coffee house
still open, near midnight —its storefront windows
misted over … You'll meet someone he said
and I piled out of the car and stepped inside
 —a bustling smoky hangout, loud music
and I made my way along an aisle
only to be stopped by a young woman
who invited me to take a seat

and there were two mugs of hot coffee
on the table in front of her
It looks like there's already someone else here
I said, and she said *I saw you come in*
and I ordered a coffee for you

The Next Morning

That woman in the diner
led me on a brisk walk the next morning
in the darkness of this sleepy town to the bridge
and down a slope along the Bow River to
a bunkhouse cabin, and we woke her friend
who ran the boat rentals

Later that day I was working for him

Much later, I also met two young women
from Manchester, and guided them
back down to the cabin by the river

We drank red wine
bundled up in wool Hudson's Bay blankets
lit a fire in the wood stove and talked
and laughed till daylight began to break
over the town's rooftops

I fell asleep thinking this was
a lot like falling in love

The Outhouse

remembering Thomas Merton

The outhouse rested all by itself
on a rise just above the river
a few feet from the cabin
perched there like a broken down
car nobody wanted anymore

but it was a room with a view
with that tiny sliver of a moon opening
carved out in the cedar boards

and sitting in there I could watch
dawn break over the nearby bridge
and the town rouse in the milky darkness
and see a blanket of mist lift from the water

or I could study a wily spider leap
across its web in a high corner of planked
boards to feast on an intruder cursing
the heavens for its unfortunate missteps

or be reminded of Thomas Merton
writing about the outhouse at the hermitage
at the Abbey of Gethsemani
and how each morning the monk stepped
cautiously inside, eyes searching warily
for 'king snake' and address it formally
as if neither of them had any business being there

I could spy the beginnings
of a day, feel it pull back the blankets
of the night, and move into the quiet rhythms
that define everything that we will take on

and I wondered is this what the poet monk
was telling us when he said he marries
the silence of the forest and openly offers
to embrace its sweet dark warmth

The Bathtub

That day we boiled up river water in pans
and kettles and pots, and we dragged
an old porcelain claw-foot bathtub
into the cabin, first emptying it
of pine needles and leaves
then carefully filled the tub
with the hot water

the two of us, then, one after the other
stripped and stepped into its steamy
warmth, and sat down in the bare-bulb glow
of this place in the woods, my first bath
in maybe weeks, cross-legged
opposite this woman, a stranger only
a few days ago, and we talked

and talked till we didn't notice the water
was getting cold

The Kiss

That morning in the diner I read
the story in the paper about
Pierre Trudeau being sworn in
as Prime Minister, and showed
the headlines to my British girlfriend
with some delight, but she shrugged
saying this was all so boring

then I told her how a friend of mine
managed to plant a kiss on Trudeau's cheek
at a rally in Toronto a month ago

my girlfriend rolled her eyes

Later that day I hiked alone
into the woods and climbed high above the town
to rest and read in open sunlight
despite a sudden chill in the still air
and at one point when I was beginning
to doze off, I glanced up
and there 10 feet away from me —
a red fox, its grizzled coat
buff neck and black-tipped tail
glowed in the afternoon light and
I watched it slip silently out of sight

and when I tracked down the slope
to the town, back to the cabin
eager to share the sight of this fox
I was met with a message
— the photograph of Trudeau
torn from *The Globe & Mail*
tacked to the wooden door
with three words penned across the picture
I'm sorry and the distinct smudge
of a red lipstick smooch
on the Prime Minister's cheek

Clean Beds in the Hotel

Having made a few bucks helping out
with the boat rentals at the cabin
one of the English girls
took me shopping for underwear and socks
— I still only possessed a thin backpack
with books and pencils

my only clothes the ones I wore

We also moved from the cabin
with its outhouse and *Canadian Tire* catalogue
to the *Cascade Inn* on the main drag

We checked in, showered
ordered room service
watched television
lounged

and listened to the news
first time in a week

Good Friday, April 12, 1968

Of course, it was raining
—it rained Good Friday
all through my Catholic upbriging
and there I was, standing on the porch
of the cabin, the spring storm streaming
through the pinewood, and onto the river
and the canoes alongside the shore
red and green, almost cheerful
under the dark sky

the two English girls wrote postcards
to friends back home, and the kettle whistled
on the stove, and I heard someone
scramble for the brown teapot

we were that day all so domesticated
watching the rain come down hard

yet deep down I wanted to get back
to the highway, find my way to the coast
though I knew not a soul there — just an idea
and again, I had nothing in the way
of money, and no real plan

I stood on the porch, the wind picking up
so I flipped up my collar to shelter my face
and strangely thought I should
go to Mass on Sunday

I kept such thoughts to myself
I wasn't sure of anything —

Good Friday and all

Lunar Eclipse April 13, 1968

We scrambled to the rooftop
of the Cascade Inn to watch the lunar eclipse
—the moon blood red in the dark sky
as it hovered over Banff and the river
like some unfamiliar relative or friend
you don't recognize in an old family album
of distant aunts and uncles and cousins long dead

and the woman I was with said the moon
was in Libra — and that was my sign
and apparently, this meant great things
for my bladder and kidneys

not really a concern of mine, as we sat
drinking red wine and talking, and I told my friend
in Luke's gospel the apostle said
There will be signs in the sun, moon, and stars

and how ancient societies believed
the lunar eclipse was a demon swallowing
the Moon and this beast could be chased away
by throwing stones and curses at it

and my friend shook her head and said no
it was really an archaic belief — the eclipse
was an age-old argument between
the sun and the moon, and it was a time
to set aside old feuds, lay them to rest

I told her I barely knew her
— we had nothing to resolve

Angels on Easter Sunday, April 14, 1968

Dawn, and I took the trail
to the Bow River Bridge and as I walked
I spotted a lone car approaching, a family
driving slowly into town — two young daughters
wearing Easter hats sitting at the back
under the sweep of the big window of the Chrysler
and they turned and stared at me
and I waved, and they smiled or giggled
— they must've been seven or eight
maybe on their way to Sunday mass
with their mother and father
and I trucked along, alone in silence
as the day was opening up
and I wasn't sure where I was going
for nothing was open and there were few
cars out, and almost nobody to be seen
but maybe it was just the quiet I needed
or likely the faces of these young girls
and it got me thinking about how
for Thomas Merton Easter Sunday was
That great silence, an immense tranquility
and a clean taste in the soul
the taste of heaven ...

Magpie

> *"Magpie! You old coyote in the sky ... "*
> — Ian Tyson

The man in the hooded parka told me
every chance he got he reached
for his .22 rifle that he kept by the kitchen door
and stepped calmly outside into his backyard
and shot one Magpie a day

and sure, he could shoot Starlings and Crows
and Pigeons and Brown-headed Cowbirds
and Blackbirds but it was the magpie
that annoyed him

told me this at a coffee shop on the main drag
cussing at nearly every other word—

I finally piped in and said they were beautiful creatures
— these black and white birds with a long
iridescent greenish black, wedge-shaped tail

and right away he fired back that they were harbingers
of doom, vermin that stole songbird
eggs and nestlings and besides, they were noisy

I reminded him Cheyenne and Algonquin legend
said the magpie was a friend of the hunter-gatherer
and in China, it was the symbol
of happiness, foretelling and good fortune

and he waved that off declaring the magpie
to be the devil that sat on the cross of Jesus
and unlike the dove, it never bothered
to catch the tears of Christ

It did no good arguing — the man
in the hooded parka would keep on loading his rifle
in the kitchen, had even started keeping count

Cold Morning on the Bow River

The rain turned to sleet but only after
we had paddled not all that far out into the river
that cold morning, our hands stiffened
in the icy weather — the only sound, the dip
and rise of our paddles in the crisp air
yet we moved with grace and ease
sitting hunched in the canoe, hoods up
maybe feeling dwarfed by the Lodgepole pines
and Englemann spruce, and the gray bleakness
of the wooded shoreline now brightened
with the first wildflowers, and I swear
I could hear Gary Snyder's raspy voice
in the poems *Hills beyond rivers, willows in a swamp,*
a gentle valley reaching far inland…The watching boat
*has floated off the page…*and there we were
sailing beyond the tarred-roof of the cabin
and now my friend was suddenly spinning
a story that I wished would quit, his voice
echoing sharply in the stillness of the day
as the sun desperately fought to untangle
itself from the clouds like a deer fly
struggling to exit a spider's web
and that's when I told him to stop
and he was in mid-sentence as we both
looked up, and standing there
15 feet from us was a black bear as round
and burnished as a sumo wrestler
and we promptly set down our paddles
let the canoe drift quietly in the dark water
but the bear never bothered to look up—
it cared more about chomping
down the dandelions, and so we pushed off
leaving behind all the symbolism of an animal
that represented strength, family, vitality
courage and health and I told my friend
how Snyder once boasted of bears in his backyard
and noticed one rooting around in his kitchen

at 6:30 one morning scarfing up vegetables
he had left in a compost bucket, and the poet
quipped that it was all Ok — *It's only when
they try to break into the refrigerator
that there's a problem.*

Back Country

For Gary Snyder

Why I slipped that book into my knapsack
and took it with me across the country
I'll never know — I had picked it up
at Marty Ahvenus' The Village Bookstore
at 29 Gerard Street in Toronto before I left

I knew nothing about Snyder
but the cover on the New Directions paperback
caught my attention: this wide-angle black
and white snapshot of the tips of trees
stretching like some gangly teenager
waking up under a wilderness sky

I heard the poet had been a fire lookout
and on the trail-crew in Yosemite
and knew he had nurtured
a deep interest in Zen Buddhism
and took his Japanese bride
to live in the Sierra Nevada range
to seek the pure wonder of the back country
the same lyric romanticism that once drove
the likes of Wordsworth
into the rolling Lake Country fields
but I was likely naive and wrong
about this— and yet the language
spoke to me, and prompted me to peer up
at the dark sky over Banff, and like him
find Jupiter and Venus so close together
like two wide-eyed innocents sitting
in hope and side by side in a park
ready for the right moment

or times when I'd make
my way back in the rain to the cabin
along the Bow River at the edge of town
and spot the blue smoke rise

in the cold air from the woodstove
and marvel at how it curled and twisted
and spiraled like the dark ink-dipped
brushstroke lettering of Zen calligraphers

Last Morning

It was hard leaving — those days
we met and stayed at the cabin
on the Bow River, mornings
when we would glide in the canoe
in the glassy black water of the river
and I'd watch her arms in perfect rhythm
of mine as we paddled in silence
and the surprise of finding nests
of cliff swallows under the bridge
or once at dawn spying a copper brown
bull elk ambling across the bridge to do
some window shopping in nearby stores

It was hard leaving — we had nothing
in common really except the laughter
but the river was where we were silent
where we harboured all feeling
and the last morning I was there
I washed her hair in the cold river —

that smile and blue eyes and long wet
braids, and body shivering
as she raced back up the hill to the cabin

Salmon Arm

An encyclopedia salesman took me
as far as Salmon Arm and cruised
along the shore of the lake yammering
the whole time, never letting me
get in a word edgewise, and invited me
to check out the name of the town
in the set of encyclopedias sprawled
across the back seat
of his baby blue Ford Falcon
thought if he took me
to the railway station,
I could catch
a night train to Vancouver
even offered to pay my way
I thanked him but declined
yet he still drove me to the station
and when we arrived, he reached
into the back seat for the right volume
and opened the page to Salmon Arm
and started reading how this town
sat on the shore of Salmon Arm Bay
surrounded by a lush rolling hillside
and had a railway station that saw
the likes of circus companies
with boxcars of wild animals
and how the original station was so close
to the water, it flooded in the spring
but this one with this sloped roof
was the place that bade farewell
to the town's young men who went off to war
and also in 1951 Princess Elizabeth
stopped for ten minutes to be given
a bouquet of flowers, and for decades
there was a photograph of that moment
on the wall near the entrance of the station

Before he left me at the big wooden doors
he flipped me his card and said if I ever got a job
and needed a set of encyclopedias
he'd be my man, no matter where I lived
— they'd arrive in the mail, but if I wanted
to take even one volume right now
at least the one with Salmon Arm
he'd hand it over to me for a buck

I counted out four quarters
scooped from my pockets

Cash for a Day's Work

Twelve of us huddled in the back
of three pickup trucks to be driven
to an industrial complex on the outskirts
of Vancouver with a job of moving equipment
and sweeping a parking lot, cash for a day's work
and I sat on the cargo bed of this bumpy
black Ford and held on for dear life as it swerved
in and out of traffic until it finally pulled up
to a collection of long low warehouses
and there I was handed a broad contractor's broom
and went to work — the whole time counting
up the dollars I'd earn, figuring
I'd finally get a hot meal, buy a toothbrush
and who knows what, never realizing I was sweeping
so fast and hard that a man with a white shirt
and a clipboard noticed me, and tapped me
on the shoulder and offered me a full-time job
 — I smiled and told him I just needed cash
to get back home, but politely thanked him
Still, he handed me a business card, said
if I changed my mind, I could show up tomorrow
on my own, not with this crew, and I promised
I'd consider it though knew there was no chance at all
 — I simply needed a little cash right away
I needed to keep going

Fifteen years later I came across his card
in a suitcase among ink-stained notebooks
faded old photographs, hotel receipts
and letters, and for a good laugh
I dialed the number

Looking for Jimi in Vancouver

After I woke in a basement apartment
just off Granville and stepped out with
a woman I met the night before
she asked if I would go with her
on that warm spring day to track down
Jimi Hendrix's grandmother on East Hastings
I tagged along wondering why
we were doing this, but I was curious
and we made our way down near the docks
to find if she was home and we knocked
on the door but a neighbour told us
she wasn't home, as a matter of fact
she was probably away — they hadn't seen her
for about a week now and so I thought
we were heading back but my new friend
said she might be at work at a steak house
over on Union, a place where Louis Armstrong
and Duke Ellington and Billie Holiday
had once played, but I told her I had
to get down to the train station —
I was heading home to Muskoka
and had to pick up money my father had wired
and she told me she'd let me know if
she found Jimi Hendrix's grandmother —
better still if she found Jimi there
for he'd always go out of his way
to visit her, always did, ever since
he was a young kid in pursuit of
a new pair of pants, or a new pair of shoes
but I had to catch a train
and I always wondered

*P.S. In September my friend sent me a postcard
saying Jimi Hendrix had just played at Vancouver's
Pacific Coliseum, and his grandmother, Nora,
ditched her front row seats to sit at the back
because the music was too loud*

Going Home

Nearly every night I traipsed back late
to a flat off 4th Street— home of a street musician
and collapsed on the floor, a few of us
sprawled there as dawn was inching its way past
the curtains, a night of smoking up
and singing, and it troubled me
after all the silence in those moments
on the highway, or kneeling in a canoe
on the Bow River as the sun was coming up
or nestling in a booth at an all-night
diner on a road at the edge of a strange town
all of that now had slipped away
like a balloon with a happy face
out of a child's grip — all that silence
Thomas Merton called a prayer
the thing that liberates you
that wordless invocation
that comes with seeing, with paying
attention, with being alert

All of that was behind me
and I went back to the street
found my way down to the railway station
took the first train home, three days
crossing the country back through
the Rockies, and slept as the forests
and lakes and towns rushed by
without ever noticing me

"having my own sun and moon and stars and a little world all to myself..."— Henry David Thoreau

Abbey of Notre-Dame du Lac

I headed east with a high school friend
and as we neared Montreal, I flattened out
the road map on my lap to search
a scattering of towns and villages
in the dim dashboard light and realized
we weren't far from a place to stay, something cheap
the Trappist monastery at Oka

— nearing midnight, we rang the bell
and waited for a sleepy guesthouse brother
to unlock the door and silently wave us in
before leading us down polished corridors
and up staircases to two rooms
side by side and nodded and bade us goodnight
and we were there in a 19th century
Cistercian monastery in the heart of Quebec

and soon the bells chimed, calling the monks for Vigils
and I unfastened the tall windows to the night
the grace of spring air filtering the room
and a buttery half-moon slumbered
just above the tall Lombardy poplars
and I pulled on my jeans and coat
then hurriedly tracked my way back
along dimly-lit corridors to the sanctuary
to see the monks streaming, white and black robes
into the choir, their first words of the day
a low rhythmic chant and the unmistakable hush
of timed and breathless silences — psalms
in the cloistered morning

remembered Merton's words about Vigils
at the Abbey of Gethsemani when after choir
he paused outside in the magical stillness
suddenly realizing the whole valley was alive
with singing crickets — this universal treble
going up to God out of the fields
and lifting effortlessly
like the incense of evening prayer

Miscou Island

We took the cable ferry to the island
but first, we had to take it to Shippigan Island
and wait for the one to Miscou
and when it came, I sat back in the car
feeling the windy sea breeze through
the rolled down windows
on this two-ferry ride into the Gulf of St. Lawrence

my friend had family there —
aunts and cousins waiting at the docks
a collection of old Chevys, rugged short men
with hands like bulky twisted ropes
and smiling women with winged spectacles
and flowered kerchiefs, and children
darting in and around the cars
these long lost relatives ready to lead us deep
into the flat, bleak, and boggy landscape
that Cartier stumbled upon after crossing
the ocean in 1534

our car, navigating narrow dirt roads
driving past ramshackle salt-sprayed shanties
hugging the coastline, and catching glimpses
of sandy white beaches and stretches
of open fields with stunted trees

and it wasn't long before
they were telling us how the place
was haunted, a cousin recounting tales
of a ghostly square-rigged barque that went down
just off Shippigan about 1800 and all hands
perished except for a cabin boy who swam
to shore, but died a few days later

and once how an uncle of his was
out fishing for herring and looked up
and suddenly there was this shapeless ball

of fire resting on a treacherous reef
all lit up and moving — this three-masted
full-rigged spectre — its wind-swept
sails wrapped in flames

I joined my friend's cousins
packed a few beers and left the car
and we all walked down to the bay
to see for ourselves but night fell
and we lost interest, indeed forgot why
we were there in the first place —

besides the wind was picking up
and it was getting cold
and we had run out of beer

Clam Digger

on Prince Edward Island

I picked my way past clumps of clapboard
shacks at Tea Hill, and finally down to the ocean
to sit and do nothing, kill some time before
my friend woke and before we got back on the road
and a gray mist covered the shore and water
and through it, I noticed a young woman edge
a path along the mudflats of the shoreline
and she was carrying a bucket and a clam fork
and she would settle down from time to time
on the sand, her body arched and taught as she dug
for white soft-shelled clams and there were moments
when the mist was so dense, she would disappear
then suddenly reappear, a ghostly shape emerging
and dissolving again in the still sea-salt air
and finally, she was closer and told me today
wasn't such a good day, the near-empty yellow bucket
supporting her claim but she was back on her knees
the sun now straining in the gray swirling air
and we talked and she said such mornings
were an exercise in patience and smiled
and was off again, disappearing along the shore
— traces of her coming and going
there and gone again, having slipped away
before I wondered if she was there at all

Ride Back

The ride back home was a problem —
my high school buddy became increasingly annoyed
at having to pay for gas and meals
though he agreed to that from the start

finally when we stopped for fuel
outside the hillside Rimouski, I hitched a ride
with someone at the gas pumps
and he drove me into town and dropped
me off on the main drag

I settled down at the long sweep
of the lunch counter at Woolworth's
for a bowl of chicken noodle soup
and two slices of white bread
and read the *Gazette*

A woman at a nearby stool
with a pack of Players tucked neatly
in next to a tea saucer
looked over and asked why
the pope was in the news
having seen his picture
above the fold

I told her he was reaffirming
his ban on contraception
in the encyclical *Humanae Vitae*

She took a long silent drag
on her cigarette, and with eyebrows raised
gazed at the teacup in front of her
then turned to me and scowled

Qu'est-ce qu'il sait sur le fait d'avoir des bébés ?

The Snapshot

Stowed away in my backpack and slipped
into Walden was a snapshot of her —
the woman I had split up with 11 months ago
— there we were resting on a beach
at Toronto's Hanlan's Point, donning
castoff army jackets, both rumpled
from a sleepless night under the stars
and beside us the remains of a campfire
that had burned all night
fed mostly by scavenged driftwood

Outside Rivière de Loup
in road side diner on the south shore
of the St. Lawrence I studied the photograph
letting the tea go cold in the mug
on the counter

and maybe there was something
in my manner that caught the interest
of the man next to me at the counter
because much later after I gathered up
my things and swung my backpack
over my shoulder, and hurried out
and down the road, this same man
from the diner pulled up ahead
alongside the road and I raced to his car
and settled down inside, and he smiled
and handed me the picture and said
Did you forget this intentionally?

Leaving Quebec City

I slumped in the backseat of a car
headed for Quebec City — jammed in
with twin boys, six years old, both asleep
all the way to the Old City —

and soon after went on foot to Rue du Trésor
where artists plied their talents
— searching for another friend, a busker
who played the flute, an unmistakable fellow
with a long, flowing blond beard

and when I asked of his whereabouts
it led me to a nearby house
and I knocked on the door and knocked again
till I heard someone inside and finally
the bearded flutist opened up, and was standing
before me —one wrist cut and bleeding profusely
a single razor blade landing at my feet
his face sullen and streaming with tears

He fell into my arms, and I led him back
inside to the bathroom, tightened a washcloth
around his wrist, rifled through the cabinets
found some band-aids, and for a long
time after he said nothing at all but over
the hours and days following, the tale of betrayal
by his girlfriend dominated the talk
till we finally packed up, caught a lift to Montreal

The Monk and the Singer

The ride I picked up in Montreal
was from a Catholic priest heading back
to Cornwall and we talked baseball and politics
but soon it came around to religion
and finally, to Thomas Merton
and he told me of the Kentucky monk's fascination
with Joan Baez, and how a friend of his
had seen the folk singer
at the Abbey of Our Lady of Gethsemani
just before Christmas, 1967 — she had gone
up to the hermitage, and Merton was surprised
to spot her running along in the rain
through the ruins of the tobacco farm
long black hair flying in the cold wind
and she stepped into the cabin
to warm up beside the fire, to drink tea
and eat goat-milk cheese and toast and honey
and Merton read poems from the summer
and Baez played one side of a new record
and the monk finally got up the nerve
to ask if she would take off her shoes
because he hadn't seen
a woman's bare foot in years

Among Saints

I set out along the ditch-line road outside Napanee
that swarmed with bright cornflowers and hollyhocks
and daylilies and noticed in a ragged field
the charred remains of a barn
yet delicate pastel-red wild roses
eagerly clambered their way up one side
and through an open window

I could've stayed there last night
had I known about the place

I found shelter in a church basement
bedding down in a storage room alongside
broken religious statues — Mother Mary
missing a right hand, a headless St Joseph
and forlorn St. Jude, the saint my mother
always prayed to, figuring he was the saint
of hopeless causes, and I was numbered
among them, and Jude hovered over me
the whole night — his left eye looked like
it had taken a beating — still I fell asleep
feeling entirely whole and intact
restored in my faith and knew soon
a car would emerge in the glistening wake
of the highway and whisk me away

The Poet in Moonlight

Nothing better than walking in the summer
from Spadina and College to High Park
or stopping at dusk at the green grocers
along Roncesvalles when it was a little cooler
sometimes joining friends for beer

but pacing the highway and praying
for a ride was frustrating and walking
was pointless — strange towns and villages
lay hundreds of miles ahead
like an open corridor, just the sky
and the road and me

I preferred to lay back well off the road
and take in the swarm of light in a dark sky
as Thoreau says *having my own sun and moon
and stars and a little world all to myself*

yet soon I wearied of reading
such dizzying words in the well-thumbed
green covered paperback I carried with me
 —especially when he went on
how *the poet who walks in moonlight
is conscious of a tide in his thought*

My only thought —
someone please pick me up

The Dog

The fields near Prescott glowed with a light frost
in the early morning, and I rubbed
my hands together, and felt my feet moving
to keep warm, and that's when I spotted
this tiny black and white dog tearing out
from a farmer's laneway to the road
just as a green pickup was rounding
the corner, and it was all over
in a couple of seconds —

the dog lay under the truck, both the driver
and I nudged its limp and slightly heavy
body out to the gravelly edge
of the road, and we hovered over it
not knowing what to do

and that's when we heard the farmer
hobbling along the laneway that led straight
back to his house and the big green barn

It surprised me that he didn't say anything
— the old man slowly knelt down
beside his dog, lifted it gently, and held it close
to his chest and whispered

and after a while, the man with the truck
helpless and fatigued of apologizing over and over again
finally got back behind the wheel and drove away

I found myself alone now with the old farmer
—a widower — and the two of us marched back
to the house where he handed me a shovel
and asked if I wouldn't mind helping him

Later the farmer drove me down the road
so, I'd have a better chance of getting a lift

and left me there, my backpack now
bulging with apples and cinnamon buns

At a Loss for Words

In the downpour, I looked for shelter
on the porch of an abandoned house
on the other side of a twisted and forsaken
barbed wire fence and I settled down
on the verandah to wait out the storm

and when the rain stopped
the bats darted out from under
the sagging eaves of the house
to dive and zigzag into the twilight

I fell asleep, eyes fixed on the hypnotic
stream of passing cars—
it might've been the best night's sleep

I woke with the sun rising over the low-lying hills
and discovered a silver bicycle lying in the grass
a few feet from the building

lifted it from the tall weeds
and straddled it —the tires still good
and began to pedal it down a stony old lane
that led from the front of the weather-beaten
farmhouse to a ruined apple orchard

If I could've remembered a simple refrain
from any Broadway musical, I might've roused
these languorous forgotten trees awake
and made them dance with me as I rode
a crooked path to celebrate the morning light

Big Man on Main Street

for Happy Farmer Humphrey, Wrestling Legend

Some would say they'd never seen
a man that huge but I recognized him
as he swaggered past afternoon shops
in Brockville as big as a buffalo

the kids chasing after him, some
struggling to dangle from his beefy arms
while others leapt like crazed hyenas onto his back
and he swept them away like flies
— he was a walking advertisement for
that night's wrestling match

I had seen him as a boy in Bracebridge —
the same spectacle of sauntering past tourists
and shop owners and handing out
flyers for the big match, and back then
he was well over 500 pounds but now
boasted nearly 700 — the fattest man
in wrestling who tossed opponents
into the stands as easily as a man flinging
flimsy lawn chairs into the lake

I trailed after him and saw him step
into a cafe and lean up against the counter
taking up room for three or four men
and order a plate of steak and eggs
and polish it off
along with three wedges of pumpkin pie
brownies and a strawberry milkshake

all to draw attention
all for the big show that night

The next morning caught him again
this time as he rode by me in a truck
the girth of him like the shadow of mountain

enveloping the front seat, dwarfing the driver
and as he passed by, he held a straw hat
out the window to wave at me
a smile breaking like concrete
on his broad face

Meeting Thoreau at the Gas Station Diner

I gave up trying to get a ride and leaned up
against a Red Maple well off the road and fell
asleep though intermittent passing cars turning
on that bend showered me with their lights
and in the morning, I crossed over to
a gas station, borrowed the key to a dimly-lit
bathroom at the back of the building
and washed my face and arms and stared
at myself in a cracked mirror wondering
what I was doing, and why it didn't matter
—the sink was black with axle grease and
the lopsided toilet seat was split in two

I headed to the station's diner for coffee
settling on a stool at the counter, ordered toast
all I could afford, and opened
Walden: A Life in the Woods
to read: *I leave the towns behind and am lost in*
some boundless heath, and life becomes gradually
more tolerable, if not even glorious
A man sitting a ways down asked what
I was reading, and I told him it was Thoreau's classic
and he nodded like it was familiar, then picked up
his coffee mug and moved over to a seat
next to mine and said, *We need only travel enough*
to give our intellects an airing…Again Thoreau
Word for word from the book, from memory
and so, the talk went, and soon the waitress
brought over a large china dinner plate
of eggs and ham and potatoes and set it down
in front of me, courtesy of the man next to me
and he smiled then stood up, and departed
and I watched him wending his way past
parked cars in the gas station lot before
taking a path beyond the highway
and vanish into the woods

Want Someone to Love

On the outskirts of Kingston
a yellow panel truck with painted advertisements
for fireworks stopped to pick me up

I wasn't about to turn down a lift

and once inside, the man with a black
fedora and a Hawaiian shirt offered me
a joint as we barreled on down the highway
him talking a mile a minute about a crackerjack
sale he had just landed in Belleville
and that's where he was headed
and would I like to come along

and I turned and surveyed the cluttered
and piled up space with teetering pyramids
of rockets and Roman Candles and trays
of sparklers and bangers and air bombs
and jumping jacks and Pom-Pom cannons
and clearly heard him shouting
We're going to war, baby! We're going to war!
drowning out Grace Slick's booming
voice *Don't You Want Somebody to Love*

The Milky Way

I wish I had paid more attention
as a boy when my father took me
outside in the middle of the night
to show me the Milky Way —
a hazy band of light
with stars as old as the universe itself
I had woken in a humid summer night
and couldn't sleep, and so my father
took me by the hand and trotted me
out into the nearby lot, an open field
and one my one introduced me
to what he called his old friends
clusters of bright stars and told me
how his father once guided him
to the edge of Cobalt to stand
on a hill, a landscape cluttered
with the head-frames of silver mines
and took inventory of these old jewels

and now years later as a young man
shuffling along this infinite highway
I realized that as the sky darkens into night
the world above me remains
an alien alphabet
radiant and puzzling

Cartwheeling in the Rain

for Brother Paul Quenon

There I was heading for the highway
the storm starting, and I took off my glasses
rain-blurred and streaked, and I slowly
ran my hands over my wet scalp
and stood still and quiet in the road
feeling the coolness of the rain
and I thought it was a blessing
not running for cover

and years later you said you already
knew this as a child, that life was rarely
complete without a good thunderstorm
a downpour, gratifying and robust

and told me of one particular day
how the clouds broke and the sun blinked
and came alive in a wondrous shower
of sunlight and rain, and how you cartwheeled
in the summer yard and how the rain fell
straight from the sun itself

Ride to Anywhere

I set out at 6 a.m. — the town's streets
deserted, a distant car rolling silently through
a stop sign, a bathroom light burning
in a nearby house, a front door opening
and a man bending down to pick up
the morning paper

otherwise alone and walking to
the edge of Colborne in hopes of a ride west

half wondering what's the hurry
and why west, though comforted with
John Steinbeck musing he had no clue where
he was heading in his travels across America
I don't care, I'd like to go anywhere

and as I prowled the morning streets with
the sliver of the moon in a silvery blue sky
I made out the sharp outline of an old house
being torn down, its empty frame and wide
open rooms and a lone toilet sitting
like an orphan child under a starry sky

The Circus

I had just settled down in a wooden booth
in a near-empty Cobourg diner with a mug of coffee
and a slice of apple pie when I noticed
children and mothers rushing
along the street all in one direction
and I asked the cook, a former high school
English teacher, who was resting
against the counter having a smoke
where they were going and he said
it was the circus

and the two of us stepped into the street
and noted how the crowds had gathered
down near the railway station, and the cook
said *Look at that long line of railway cars*
— they're stretching like a run-on sentence
with too many nouns

Minutes later I was standing on the platform
of the station eyeing an army of stocky men
with floppy wool caps and rolled-up shirtsleeves
unload the boxcars and set up the circus
in a nearby open field, and cheers went up
when five elephants lumbered down
the sturdy ramps and past the spectators
followed by crated cages of lions and chimpanzees

then soon the big draught horses began
to ease the rods and riggings and canvas off
the railway flatcars all bearing the name
of Ringling Brothers

and I wondered about the Big Top aerialists
trampolinists, the clowns, and wild animal acts
and the Liberty horses when abruptly
a big wooden *Canadian National* boxcar door
slid open, and out popped the head

of a giraffe who possessed all the confidence
and curiosity of an ordinary tourist
wishing to catch a bit of air

The Medical Building

The first afternoon on my return
to Toronto before heading south
I rode the College streetcar
to the U of T's old Medical Building
and took the stairs two at a time
to the roof to find an old friend who worked
there as mail clerk, and we walked
in the sunshine — the roof where
Banting and Best paraded their dogs
for picture-taking before subjecting them
to experiments, and one after another
these pets perished, all in the service
for the discovery of insulin, the long
sought-after treatment for diabetes

My friend most days slouched
on a patched-up wooden chair reading alone
at a small wooden lab table
in the cavernous vacant and empty top floor
of the building, surrounded by empty
old wire cages that once housed those animals

and told me stories of Banting running short
of dogs, and being forced to snatch pets
off the street and backyards and lure
them into his lab in this building
into the cages sitting just a few feet away

all in the service of a Nobel Prize

After a while, the two scientists
ceased christening the dogs with names
— they merely became numbers

yet a photo survives of the two scientists
on the roof in August 1921 with
a lean black and white dog, Marjorie

or Dog #408

The other 407 all died before her

I wish my friend had accompanied me

Blue Wool-Knit Sweater

For K. Y.

A day never went by on the road
when I didn't wear the blue wool-knit vest sweater
she had made for me when we lived
in Toronto's Roncesvalles — it reminded me
of one Ezra Pound wore on the cover
of a paperback book of poems
and a half-century later I know
it's now somewhere in my house

and still connects me to our time together
in the rainy fall weather of Toronto
when we rode the King streetcar
to the west end — rain drops speckling
the cold windows, offering a blurred abstraction
of a city finishing its day before we got off
at High Park and walked among
greengrocers and bakeries and cafes
and wended our way back to our flat
on the second floor with a tall Maple
that stood on the front lawn and peered
into our wide front windows

I still have that sweater I took with me
riding out west in the spring after we called it quits
  — I have it somewhere

I'll find it

I also kept the book by Pound and know
exactly where it is on a shelf in my study

It still bears her turquoise-ink signature
and dedication with the message *Forever*

Epilogue: Going South

It had been years since living in Windsor
— that last time strolling with my aging Pepé
in a sunny backyard while he tended
a small garden patch of tomatoes and cucumbers
and long before at Stoney Point
and someone snapped a Kodak of him
in a straw hat riding a combine, a pipe
clenched in his mouth

and now heading to Windsor
in the back of my brother's Ford station wagon
a rolled down windy window view of the road
as we sped south from Muskoka —
my six-year-old nephew and his two younger sisters
squeezed in beside me, and when we landed
in the city, I slept on my brother's couch
started work at Chrysler's Foundry
before finding a job at *The Windsor Star*

then promptly moved out
to a dive on Riverside Drive, a room
above a bar, a broken window and
narrow dirty hallways and rarely saw
the stream of late-night prostitutes
because I worked the night desk at the paper
and didn't finish till the sun was coming up
over the blue-gray of the river

better than life on the road
tuning my radio into the Detroit Tigers
cheering them on to win the World Series
and scribbling into a notebook
about the months that had passed
hitchhiking through the Rockies
or ambling along the shore of the St Lawrence
and strangely never writing about the women
who quietly slipped out into the dark

empty hotel hallways at dawn
to leave behind the sleeping Johns

Acknowledgements

Getting someone to pick up and read your work is the biggest acknowledgement. At the top of that list is Bruce Meyer, who spent the time shaping and organizing this manuscript, and writing his introduction. He was my guide. D.A. Lockhart, who offered to publish this for Urban Farmhouse, instantly saw the value in narrowing my vision to write about this incredible journey. We talked about it endlessly over coffee at Tim Hortons near my house, or 'the office' as those who know me call it. The list of thankyous is endless, and I owe by gratitude for so many who have supported my work. To name a few, let me include Peter Hrastovec, Ted Kloske, Howard and Jeannette Aster, John B. Lee, Vanessa Shields, André Narbonne, Rosemary Sullivan, Douglas MacLellan, Betsy Struthers, Emily Lockhart, Phil Hall, Laurence Hutchman, Terry Ann Carter, Roger Bryan, Brian Fox, Mary Ann Mulhern, Christopher Lawrence Menard, Micheline Maylor, Susan McMaster, and Karen Mulhallen. Of course, I can't forget the patience of my own family —they listen when they don't have to. Especially my daughter, Elise.

About the Author

Marty Gervais (author) from the summer of roadtrip

Marty Gervais, the City of Windsor's inaugural Poet Laureate, and now Poet Laureate Emeritus, is a Canadian poet, photographer, journalist, and teacher. He has won many literary awards including the prestigious Toronto's Harbourfront Festival Prize for his contributions to Canadian letters and emerging writers, the Milton Acorn People's Poetry Award, and the City of Windsor's Mayor's Award. Gervais, whose book **The Rumrunners**, was a Canadian bestseller, is also the recipient of 16 Western Ontario Newspaper Awards for journalism and was given the Queen's Jubilee Medal.

CPSIA information can be obtained
at www.ICGtesting.com
Printed in the USA
BVHW052000240722
642543BV00001B/60

9 781988 214481